Formula 1™

Published by Ladybird Books Ltd
A Penguin Company
Penguin Books Ltd, 80 Strand, London, WC2R 0RL, UK
Penguin Books Australia Ltd, Camberwell, Victoria, Australia
Penguin Books (NZ), 67 Apollo Drive, Rosedale, North Shore
0632, New Zealand (a divison of Pearson New Zealand Ltd)
www.ladybird.com

Photography credits:
© Martin Trenkler
With thanks to Renault, Williams, Bridgestone, Force India, Red Bull, BMW Sauber, Toro Rosso, Toyota, Brawn GP.

ISBN: 9781409302889
10 9 8 7 6 5 4 3 2 1
Printed in Italy

OFFICIAL ANNUAL 2010

CONTENTS

INTRODUCTION

Who could ever forget the nail-biting finish to the 2008 Grand Prix™ season?

The final race in Brazil was all set up for the perfect finish, as local hero Felipe Massa took on Lewis Hamilton for the F1™ racing crown. And, of course, as we all know, Hamilton held on to take the championship by just one point. Incredible stuff – but who's to say that 2009 will be any different?

Could this be the year that the stranglehold of the big four – Ferrari, Williams, Renault and McLaren – is finally broken? Will the likes of Red Bull Racing or Force India finally break their Grand Prix™ victory duck? And will one of the sport's up-and-coming drivers such as Sebastian Vettel be able to make his mark?

There have been quite a few changes to F1™ racing this season and many are designed to help the smaller teams compete with the big boys on a much more even basis. And from the fans' point of view, that makes for even more exciting races!

Among the changes is a return to slicks, a type of tyre that has very little tread on it and that should make the cars perform even better. Although with other rule changes meaning less grip is available, the drivers may have to ease up on the throttle a bit as they blast through the corners!

Also new is the Kinetic Energy Recovery Systems (KERS). OK, so it sounds like something out of Doctor Who, but many constructors have decided to introduce this clever system. It stores up the energy generated when the car brakes, and then releases it, bit by bit, to boost the car's power. How brilliant is that?

The year 2009 also sees the unveiling of another new track, the Yas Marina Circuit in Abu Dhabi, which is all part of Formula One™ racing's plan to keep spreading the sport to all four corners of the globe.

Enjoy the racing!

For all the latest news and top interviews, make sure you're a regular visitor to the official Formula One™ racing's website – www.formula1.com

6

THE POINTS SYSTEM

Here's how the points are shared out at a Grand Prix™. The points count towards both the Drivers' and the Constructors' World Championships:

1st PLACE:	10 points	5th PLACE:	4 points
2nd PLACE:	8 points	6th PLACE:	3 points
3rd PLACE:	6 points	7th PLACE:	2 points
4th PLACE:	5 points	8th PLACE:	1 point

THE DRIVERS' WORLD CHAMPIONSHIP 2008

1	Lewis Hamilton	98
2	Felipe Massa	97
3	Kimi Räikkönen	75
4	Robert Kubica	75
5	Fernando Alonso	61
6	Nick Heidfeld	60
7	Heikki Kovalainen	53
8	Sebastian Vettel	35
9	Jarno Trulli	31
10	Timo Glock	25
11	Mark Webber	21
12	Nelson Piquet Jnr	19
13	Nico Rosberg	17
14	Rubens Barrichello	11
15	Kazuki Nakajima	9
16	David Coulthard	8
17	Sebastien Bourdais	4
18	Jenson Button	3
19	Giancarlo Fisichella	0
20	Adrian Sutil	0
21	Takuma Sato	0
22	Anthony Davidson	0

THE CONSTRUCTORS' WORLD CHAMPIONSHIP 2008

1	Ferrari	172
2	McLaren-Mercedes	151
3	BMW Sauber	135
4	Renault	80
5	Toyota	56
6	STR-Ferrari	39
7	Red Bull-Renault	29
8	Williams-Toyota	26
9	Honda	14
10	Force India-Ferrari	0
11	Super Aguri-Honda	0

TRUE OR FALSE?

We've trawled through Formula One™ racing's archive to come up with a fiendish farrago of facts. Your job is to decide which ones are true, and which are false and out to trip you up! Circle the right answers.

1 British drivers have won more Drivers' World Championships than any other country. **T F**

2 In the 1970s, a team called Tyrrell raced with a car that had six wheels. **T F**

3 The late, great Ayrton Senna was from Argentina. **T F**

4 In 2010 it's rumoured that South Korea could stage its first ever Grand Prix. **T F**

5 This is a photograph of Silverstone, venue for the 2009 British Grand Prix. **T F**

6 Nick Heidfeld, Sebastian Vettel and Nico Rosberg are all French racing drivers. **T F**

7 Lewis Hamilton won the 2008 Drivers' Championship driving at Williams. **T F**

8 Bingo Scorer is an anagram of Nico Rosberg. **T F**

9 He may have been pipped to the Championship by Lewis Hamilton, but Felipe Massa actually won more Grands Prix than the Brit in 2008. **T F**

10 The Suzuka and Fuji circuits are both in Japan. **T F**

11 Drivers must complete 100 laps in the Monaco Grand Prix. **T F**

12 A marshal waving a red and yellow flag means that drivers need to be extra careful as the track is slippery. **T F**

13 In 2008, the Force India team was made up of Adrian Sutil and Robert Kubica. **T F**

14 Alain Prost is the only Frenchman to win the Drivers' World Championship. **T F**

15 Born in 1973, Giancarlo Fisichella is the old man of the Grand Prix scene. **T F**

16 In 1976 the British Grand Prix was a dead heat between Britain's James Hunt and the Austrian great Niki Lauda. **T F**

17 There has never been a Grand Prix held in Africa. **T F**

18 Heikki Kovalainen, Mika Hakkinen and Kimi Räikkönen are all from Iceland. **T F**

19 First place on the starting grid is called pole position. **T F**

20 Ferrari, Monza and Giancarlo Fisichella are all linked by Italy. **T F**

THE FORMULA ONE™ GLOSSARY

Formula One™ racing isn't just about tearing around a track at over 300km/h – it's got a whole language all of its own, too! So, to help you follow the coverage, and understand why bottoming isn't rude, and blistering isn't as painful as it sounds, we've come up with a list of some of the sport's more common terms – and some of the more unusual!

AERODYNAMICS
To make F1 cars go as fast as possible, the teams spend a fortune making them aerodynamic. This means making sure the car is designed and shaped so that there is as little wind resistance as possible.

APEX
The middle point of the inside line around a corner on the track. The driver aims for this spot, which is the ideal racing line, allowing them to get round the corner as quickly as possible.

BALLAST
F1 cars must weigh no less than 605kg (including the driver) but they are usually made lighter than this. Ballasts are weights fixed around the car to achieve regulation weight, and may not be added or removed during the race.

BLISTERING
This is all about tyres. When they get too hot or worn out, bits of the rubber break off. What's left looks very much like a blister.

BOTTOMING
Stop sniggering at the back! Bottoming happens when the car's chassis scrapes the track as it goes round.

BRAKE BALANCE
There's a nifty little switch in the cockpit which the driver can use to alter the way the front and back brakes work. Get it right, and the car will go faster.

CAMBER
The wheels on an F1 car are never put on dead straight. They are usually set up to lean into or away from the car – this is the camber. The cars are set up like this to help them corner at higher speeds.

CARBON FIBRE
Super light, super strong, super useful! Every F1 car is now made from carbon fibre, which is a bit like plastic but with hairs of carbon added for extra strength.

CHICANE
A tricky part of the circuit that usually involves two or more corners, each going in the opposite direction. They are a real test of driver skill, and are often designed to slow cars down.

DOWNFORCE
More science – this is the aerodynamic force that pushes the car down as it goes along. Those clever designers often build a car so that it can actually use downforce to improve its handling, especially around corners.

DRAG
And yet more science – this time the aerodynamic resistance experienced by a car as it travels forward.

DRIVE-THROUGH PENALTY
If a driver commits an offence on the track, the marshals can order him to take a detour through the pit lane. The catch is that they have to slow right down to pit-lane speed before rejoining the race at the other end of the pit lane.

F.I.A.
Otherwise known as the Fédération Internationale de l'Automobile – Formula One racing's governing body.

FLAGS
See the quiz on page 16.

FORMATION LAP
This is the lap before the start of the race – you know the one, when the drivers all look like they've forgotten how to drive as they weave from one side of the track to the other! Of course, what they're really doing is warming up their cars, and their tyres in particular.

G-FORCE
Another force, this time one that the drivers feel when they corner, accelerate or brake.

GRAVEL TRAP
No, not some new method of catching slugs, but instead a safely feature on most circuits. It involves a bed of gravel that slows the car down if it comes off the track.

HAIRPIN
A very tight corner that turns back on itself. Drivers really need to drop through the gears to get through these.

JUMP-START
Drivers wait on the grid for five red lights to be switched off before they set off to start. Special sensors detect if they go before the lights are out. This is a jump-start and will earn them a time penalty.

KERS
KERS stands for Kinetic Energy Recovery Systems, and without boring you with all the details, KERS recover and store energy when the car brakes and then use this energy to make the car go even faster. Pretty good idea really!

LOLLIPOP

No, not that kind of lollipop. This is the sign on a stick held in front of the car during a pit stop to tell the driver that the car is up on jacks, so don't try and drive off!

MARSHAL

The marshals are positioned at various places round the track, and are in charge of safety. This often involves waving various coloured flags to let drivers know several things, such as if there is a hazard on the track, like a broken-down car.

OVERSTEER

Oversteer is when the back end of the car pushes out wide as the driver goes round a corner, while the front end sticks to the 'racing line'. It often makes the car look like it is going sideways.

PADDOCK

This is an area behind the pits where the drivers can relax before and after the race and hold interviews with the media. It's a no-go area for the likes of you and me!

PARC FERMÉ

In between qualifying and the actual race, all the cars are held in this secure, fenced-off area. And absolutely no one is allowed in unless supervised by a race steward.

IT'S THE PITS

The **pits** are a special area of the track by the start/finish line that's separate from the rest of the circuit. Cars come in for a

pit stop during the race. These are crucial to the outcome of a race and teams of mechanics are trained to complete them in super fast time so the car can rejoin the race as soon as possible.

It takes three mechanics to change a wheel. Using a high-speed airgun, one will remove and refit the special nut that keeps the wheel on, another will remove the old wheel, and a third will fit the new one. At the same time, two mechanics refuel the car. A good crew will complete the stop in around 7 seconds, although the fastest recorded was in 1993 when the Benetton team completed a tyre change in just 4.3 seconds!

The driver's team are in contact with the driver by radio. They may also hold up a **pit board** that gives them basic details about where they are in the race.

The **pit wall** is an area of the pits where the team's engineers sit to monitor the race on computers and TV screens.

POLE POSITION

This is the first place on the starting grid and goes to the driver who records the fastest lap time in qualifying. If they get it right, it means they can usually get to the first corner ahead of the pack, and avoid any smashes!

QUALIFYING

This takes place on the Saturday before the race and decides the positions on

12

the starting grid for the race proper. It's divided into three stages, spread over an hour, with each car allowed to do as many laps as they wish. The slowest five cars in the first two phases are eliminated and make up the back of the grid. The fastest lap of the final session takes pole position, the second-fastest second place, and so on.

RACING LINE
An imaginary line that the drivers try to keep to because in theory it's the fastest way around the circuit.

SAFETY CAR
If there's an accident or hazard on the track the race has to be slowed down, so the safety car will come out of the pits and drive in front of the leading car, and the driver is not allowed to overtake it.

SLIPSTREAMING
This is a top driving skill. The idea is to tuck in behind the car in front of you, and let that car punch a hole in the air. Your car will then have less drag and air resistance on it so that when you come up to the next corner you should have that extra bit of power you need to spring out and overtake the car in front.

'SPLASH AND DASH'
If the crew get their measurements wrong, and the car looks like it's going to run out of fuel before the end of the race, the driver may have to make an unscheduled pit stop to get just a 'splash' of fuel, before making a 'dash' to finish the race.

STOP-GO PENALTY
This penalty means the driver has to return to the pits and stop for 10 seconds before rejoining the race. The crew aren't allowed to do anything to the car during this time.

TEAR-OFF STRIPS
You may have noticed that F1 cars don't have a windscreen, which means the driver's visor gets covered in splattered bugs and other muck throughout the race. To get round this, the visor has a number of tear-off strips which the driver can remove as they become dirty.

TELEMETRY
A hi-tech system that sends information about the car back to computers in the pit garage so that engineers can monitor exactly what's going on.

UNDERSTEER
As you'd expect, this is the opposite to oversteer. This time it's the front of the car that won't go where it's supposed to, with the car pushing out wide rather than turning into the corner.

WHERE IN THE WORLD?

Formula One™ raciing is a truly global sport. Its origins may be very much based in Europe, but over the years it has spread its wings to North America, Australia and most recently Asia, too. Here's the low-down on ten of the greatest F1™ nations of all time.

GREAT BRITAIN

First Grand Prix: 1950
Great circuits: Brands Hatch, Silverstone, Donington Park
World Championships: Thirteen – Jackie Stewart (three), Jim Clark (two), Graham Hill (two), Mike Hawthorn, John Surtees, James Hunt, Nigel Mansell, Damon Hill and ▮▮▮▮▮
Anything else? Stirling Moss, who was one of the few men good enough to challenge the brilliant Fangio in the 1950s, has been described as the 'greatest driver never to win the Championship'.

USA

First Grand Prix: 1959
Great circuits: ▮▮▮▮▮ Long Beach, Watkins Glen
World Championships: Two – Phil Hill and Mario Andretti.
Anything else? In 1982 the USA became the first country to stage three Grands Prix in one season. How greedy is that?

FRANCE

First Grand Prix: 1950
Great circuits: Magny-Cours, Paul Ricard
World Championships: Four, all won by ▮▮▮▮▮
Anything else? Despite being in at the start of Formula One racing, the French Grand Prix dropped off the calendar in 2009. Sacrebleu!

BRAZIL

First Grand Prix: 1972
Great circuit: Interlagos
World Championships: Eight – Nelson Piquet (three), ▮▮▮▮▮ (three) and Emerson Fittipaldi (two).
Anything else? Surely it can't be long before Felipe Massa makes it nine world championships for Brazil?

ARGENTINA

First Grand Prix: 1953
Great circuits: Buenos Aires
World Championships: Five – take a bow ▮▮▮▮▮
Anything else? To be honest, the Argentines have been a bit of a disappointment since Fangio hung up his goggles. The best they've done is stage three Grands Prix in one season.

See if you can fill in the gaps on the map above with these words:

14

FINLAND

First Grand Prix: They've never had one!
Great circuits: There aren't any!
World Championships: Four – [redacted] (two), Keke Rosberg and Kimi Räikkönen.
Anything else? Given that there are no great circuits in Finland, we'll just have to put the country's success down to pure skill!

GERMANY

First Grand Prix: 1951
Great circuits: The Nürburging, Hockenheimring
World Championships: Seven, all won by Michael Schumacher.
Anything else? Racing legend Jackie Stewart used to call the [redacted] the 'Green Hell', as it was the most difficult and dangerous circuit going.

AUSTRIA

First Grand Prix: 1964
Great circuits: A1-Ring, Österreichring
World Championships: Four – [redacted] (three) and Jochen Rindt.
Anything else? Rindt is the only driver to have won the title after he died. He was fatally injured during practise for the 1970 Italian Grand Prix but with three races left, he had still earnt enough points to win the title.

ITALY

First Grand Prix: 1950
Great circuit: [redacted]
World Championships: Three – Alberto Ascari (two) and Nino Farina (one).
Anything else? The last time an Italian won the title was in 1953. It's the name of Ferrari that's the true King of Italian motorsport.

AUSTRALIA

First Grand Prix: 1985
Great circuit: [redacted]
World Championships: Four – Jack Brabham (three) and Alan Jones.
Anything else? The 1991 Australian Grand Prix is remembered as the shortest ever and was stopped on lap fourteen because of torrential rain.

Nürburgring
Mika Hakkinen
Monza
Indianapolis
Juan Manuel Fangio

Albert Park
Alain Prost
Niki Lauda
Ayrton Senna
Lewis Hamilton

NAME THAT FLAG

Flags are big in F1™ racing. No, we don't mean the homemade variety waved by the crowd with things like 'Lewis we love you' or 'Kubica is cute' scrawled on them in marker pen, we mean the ten flags that are used to control a race and pass instructions on to the drivers.

So, let's test your knowledge and find out if you've really been paying attention while watching the race on telly.

1

A blue flag is shown to a particular driver to:

A. Let him know a faster car is behind him and is trying to overtake.
B. Tell him it's going to rain.
C. Tell him to make a pit stop to take on more water.

2

A green flag is shown to all drivers to tell them:

A. It's time to switch to unleaded petrol.
B. It's a salad for tea.
C. A hazard has been cleared and they can continue at normal racing speed.

3

If you don't know this one, you're reading the wrong book! A chequered flag is shown to:

A. Signal the start of the race.
B. Signal the end of the race.
C. Let drivers know that there are ten laps to go.

4

When a black flag is waved at an individual driver it means:

A. Caution, you've sprung a leak.
B. Watch out for pirates.
C. Head to the pits immediately (usually because they've broken the rules).

5 A black flag with an orange disc means drivers must:

A. Put on their headlights.
B. Return to the pits because the car has a mechanical problem.
C. Watch out, there's a streaker on the track!

6 As a driver swoops through a chicane, he sees a yellow flag, which means:

A. Slow down and no overtaking, danger ahead.
B. Watch out for custard on the track.
C. There's been a pile-up in the sand.

7 A marshal is frantically waving a white flag at everyone, which means:

A. It's snowing.
B. There's a slow moving vehicle on the track, such as a safety car.
C. It's the end of the practice lap.

8 Very occasionally drivers are shown a black and white flag with diagonal halves, along with their car number, meaning that:

A. It's getting dark.
B. The driver has behaved unsportingly – carry on like that and they could be facing a black flag.
C. They should smile, as their on-board camera is beaming pictures of them across the world.

9 This time the marshal has a rather fetching red and yellow striped flag in his hand, meaning:

A. There's been a crash.
B. Just one more lap to go.
C. Be careful, the circuit is slippery.

10 There are red flags being waved all round the track because:

A. A Ferrari has just won the race.
B. The race has been stopped.
C. The driver is on the phone and they've got to return to the pits, pronto.

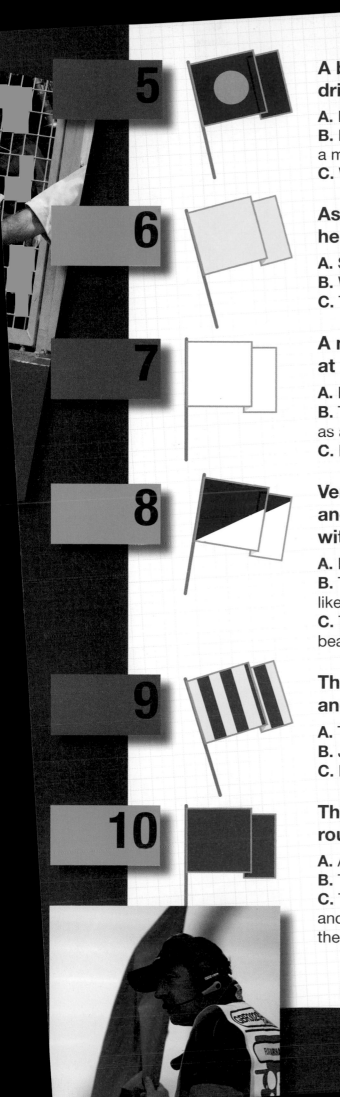

F1™ RACING BOARD GAME

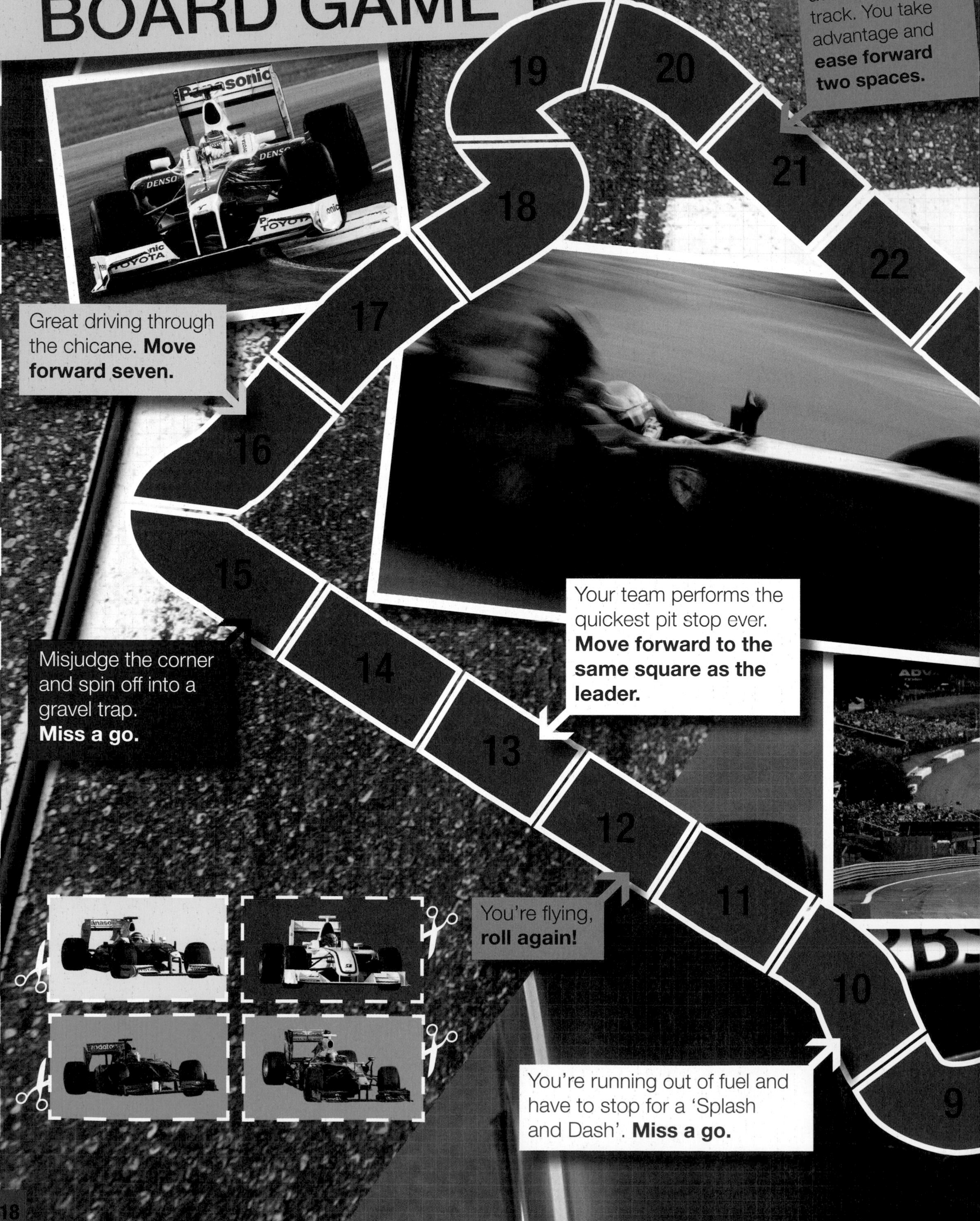

The car in front of you swerves to avoid a dog on the track. You take advantage and **ease forward two spaces.**

Great driving through the chicane. **Move forward seven.**

Misjudge the corner and spin off into a gravel trap. **Miss a go.**

Your team performs the quickest pit stop ever. **Move forward to the same square as the leader.**

You're flying, **roll again!**

You're running out of fuel and have to stop for a 'Splash and Dash'. **Miss a go.**

9
10
11
12
13
14
15
16
17
18
19
20
21
22

Who's going to win the British Grand Prix™ in 2010? With just ten laps to go, Lewis Hamilton, Fernando Alonso and Felipe Massa are neck and neck. It looks set to be one of the most incredible finishes ever. And now it's up to you to take over.

HOW TO PLAY:
Choose which driver you want to represent (no, you can't all be Lewis!), grab a die, cut out the car counters, and get going!

It's raining and you need to change your tyres. **Miss two goes.**

24

25

28

29

The marshals are now waving a yellow flag, which means slow down, no over-taking. **Take one point off your next three rolls of the die.**

26

27

30

A marshal has waved a black flag at you. **Go back five spaces.**

FINISH

START

1

2

You get stuck behind a back marker. **Miss a go.**

3

8

6

5

4

7

Brakes lock. **Miss a go.**

Skid on an oily patch, **go back two!**

THE TEAMS

Here's the low-down on all the teams taking part in the current F1™ championship. A few have been at it for years but there are also a lot of new teams trying to break into the big time, too. Who do you think will win?

RENAULT

Renault took over the old Benetton team in 2001. Before that, however, several cars had won championships using Renault engines.

Team debut: British Grand Prix 1977
This year's drivers: Fernando Alonso and Nelson Piquet Jnr
Overall Grand Prix wins: 35
Drivers' World Championships: 2
Constructors' World Championships: 2
Greatest ever drivers: Alain Prost, Fernando Alonso
Finest hour: Has to be 2005, when Alonso won Renault its first ever Drivers' World Championship.

FERRARI

Is there a more famous name in motor racing? Named after the company's founder, Enzo Ferrari, no team has won more Drivers' or Constructors' World Championships than this team.

Team debut: Monaco Grand Prix 1950
This year's drivers: Kimi Räikkönen and Felipe Massa
Overall Grand Prix wins: 209
Drivers' World Championships: 15
Constructors' World Championships: 16
Greatest ever drivers: Niki Lauda, Gilles Villeneuve, Michael Schumacher
Finest hour: Despite their long history, Ferrari's greatest success came this century with Michael Schumacher behind the wheel. He won five championships on the trot between 2000–04.

RED BULL RACING

A British-based team that used to race as Jaguar Racing. Still finding their feet in the ultra-competitive world of F1 racing.

Team debut: Australian Grand Prix 2005
This year's drivers: Mark Webber and Sebastian Vettel
Overall Grand Prix wins: 0
Drivers' World Championships: 0
Constructors' World Championships: 0
Greatest ever driver: David Coulthard
Finest hour: They're still waiting! So far just three podium finishes is all they've got to show for their efforts.

TOYOTA

Despite being a massive name in motoring, Toyota is still looking for their first Grand Prix victory.

Team debut: Australian Grand Prix 2002
This year's drivers: Jarno Trulli and Timo Glock
Overall Grand Prix wins: 0
Drivers' World Championships: 0
Constructors' World Championships: 0
Greatest ever drivers: Ralf Schumacher, Jarno Trulli
Finest hour: Just eight podium finishes so far but could 2009 be the year that Toyota roars?

WILLIAMS

One of the big names in Formula One racing, with six different drivers taking their cars to victory over the years.

Team debut: Argentina Grand Prix 1980
This year's drivers: Nico Rosberg and Kazuki Nakajima
Overall Grand Prix wins: 113
Drivers' World Championships: 7
Constructors' World Championships: 9
Greatest ever drivers: Nigel Mansell, Ayrton Senna, Damon Hill
Finest hour: There have been a few high spots but Mansell winning the championship by an incredible 52 points in 1992 was probably the most satisfying.

McLAREN

Another of the most successful teams in F1 history, the famous red and white cars dominated during the 1980s with five titles.

Team debut: Monaco Grand Prix 1966
This year's drivers: Lewis Hamilton and Heikki Kovalainen
Overall Grand Prix wins: 162
Drivers' World Championships: 12
Constructors' World Championships: 8
Greatest ever drivers: James Hunt, Niki Lauda, Alain Prost, Ayrton Senna, Mika Hakinnen
Finest hour: Last year when Lewis Hamilton became their first drivers' champion since 1999.

TORO ROSSO

Based in Italy, the team raced as Minardi between 1985–2005. They're also known as Red Bull's junior team.

Team debut: Bahrain Grand Prix 2006
This year's drivers: Sebastien Buemi and Sebastien Bourdais
Overall Grand Prix wins: 1
Drivers' World Championships: 0
Constructors' World Championships: 0
Greatest ever driver: Sebastian Vettel – and no, it's not a rule that you have to be called Sebastian to drive for this team!
Finest hour: Their one and only victory, which saw Vettel take the chequered flag at the Italian Grand Prix in 2008.

BRAWN GP

This new team was bought by the ex-team principal of Honda, Ross Brawn, after it was announced that Honda were pulling out.

Team debut: Australian Grand Prix 2009
This year's drivers: Jenson Button and Rubens Barrichello
Overall Grand Prix wins: 2
Drivers' World Championships: 0
Constructors' World Championships: 0
Greatest ever drivers: We'll have to wait and see!
Finest hour: This new team has already made their mark by winning their debut Grand Prix race, with Button coming first and Barrichello coming second. It looks like 2009 is going to be an exciting year!

BMW SAUBER

The team has bases in both Switzerland and Germany, and was formed in 2005, when BMW took over the Sauber racing team.

Team debut: South African Grand Prix 1993
This year's drivers: Robert Kubica and Nick Heidfeld
Overall Grand Prix wins: 1
Drivers' World Championships: 0
Constructors' World Championships: 0
Greatest ever driver: Jacques Villeneuve
Finest hour: They notched up their first victory at the 2008 Canadian Grand Prix thanks to Kubica. Could this be the sign of things to come?

FORCE INDIA

Another new kid on the block, the team is based at Silverstone but heavily backed by Indian money.

Team debut: Australian Grand Prix 2008
This year's drivers: Adrian Sutil and Giancarlo Fisichella
Overall Grand Prix wins: 0
Drivers' World Championships: 0
Constructors' World Championships: 0
Greatest ever drivers: Too early to say
Finest hour: Lining up on the grid for the first time ever at last year's Australian Grand Prix.

Stats correct up until the second Grand Prix™ of 2009.

THE F1™ HALL OF FAME

Here's a full list of the F1™ Drivers' Champions from the past 20 years. The eagle-eyed amongst you will soon notice that just ten drivers have shared the crown over all that time. **Will 2009 see a new name added to the roll of honour?**

1988
Ayrton Senna
90 points – Brazil
McLaren

1989
Alain Prost
76 points – France
McLaren

1990
Ayrton Senna
78 points – Brazil
McLaren

1991
Ayrton Senna
96 points – Brazil
McLaren

1992
Nigel Mansell
108 points – Great Britain
Williams

1993
Alain Prost
99 points – France
Williams

1994
Michael Schumacher
92 points – Germany
Benetton

1995
Michael Schumacher
102 points – Germany
Benetton

1996
Damon Hill
97 points – Great Britain
Williams

1997
Jacques Villeneuve
81 points – Canada
Williams

1998
Mika Hakkinen
100 points – Finland
McLaren

1999
Mika Hakkinen
76 points – Finland
McLaren

2000
Michael Schumacher
108 points – Germany
Ferrari

2001
Michael Schumacher
123 points – Germany
Ferrari

2002
Michael Schumacher
144 points – Germany
Ferrari

2003
Michael Schumacher
93 points – Germany
Ferrari

2004
Michael Schumacher
148 points – Germany
Ferrari

2005
Fernando Alonso
133 points – Spain
Renault

2006
Fernando Alonso
134 points – Spain
Renault

2007
Kimi Räikkönen
110 points – Finland
Ferrari

2008
Lewis Hamilton
98 points – Great Britain
McLaren

2009

DESIGN YOUR OWN HELMET

Crash helmets have come a long way since the days of Juan Manuel Fangio, one of the first Formula One greats. All he had to protect his head was a thin cap made of leather and a pair of flying goggles!

Gradually things improved and by the1960s helmets were at least hard and rigid. In the 1970s they had become 'full face' and included a visor too.

These days they're all tested to the limit. For instance, to make sure that the visor is safe and up to the job, it is shot at with an air rifle! And even though the pellets fizz along at 500 km/h, if they make a dent of more than 2.5mm, the visor gets chucked in the bin!

So with the safety sorted, next up is the livery, or the colours and designs that are added to the helmet. Most are painstakingly painted on by hand and usually reflect the team colours, although that's not to say that drivers don't have a few ideas of their own!

Take BMW Sauber's Nick Heidfeld, who changed his colour scheme for the start of the 2009 season. "I took my inspiration from a snowboard helmet that I saw when I was on holiday," he said. "I wanted a somewhat more aggressive look. Green makes quite a change, as none of the other F1 drivers sport a green helmet at the moment."

Or perhaps you like Red Bull's Sebastian Vettel's idea of personalizing his helmet with flashes of yellow, purple and pink?

Renault's Fernando Alonso, however, prefers red and yellow but with a pair of Aces on the back. Stylish, eh?

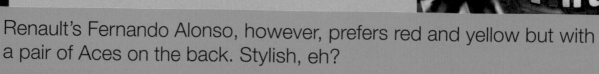

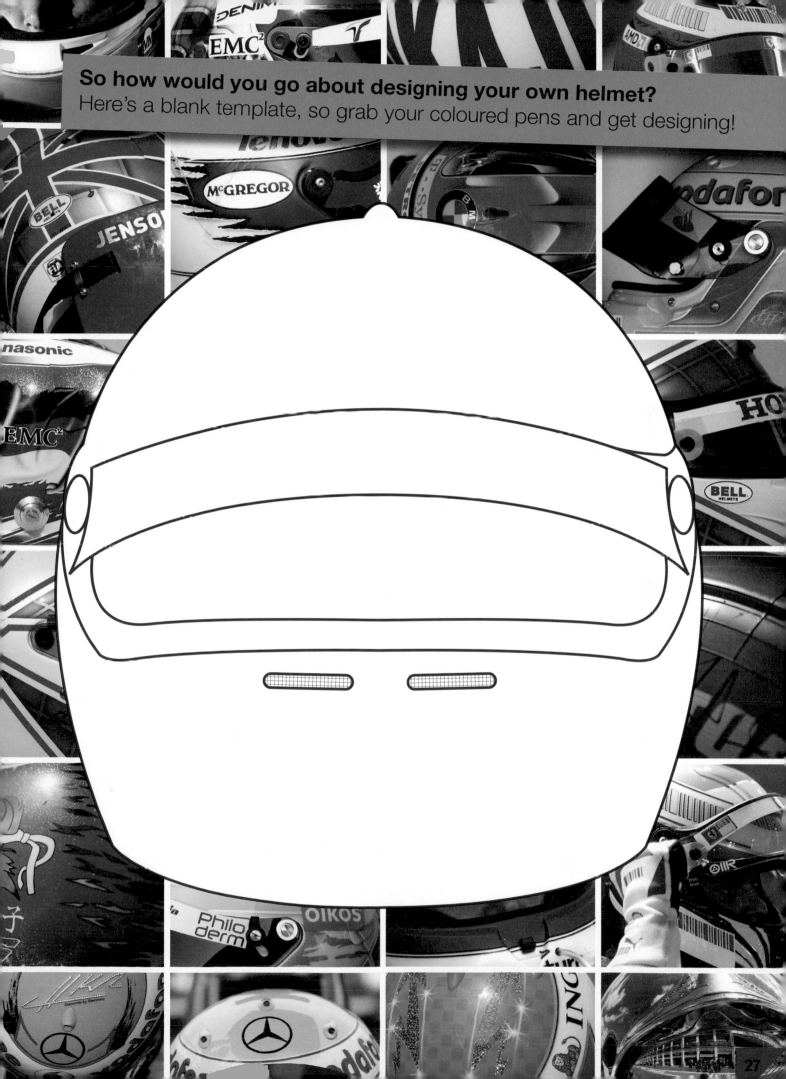

So how would you go about designing your own helmet?
Here's a blank template, so grab your coloured pens and get designing!

NAME THAT TRACK IN ONE!

OK, let's see how quickly you can recognize five of the F1™ tracks that will all feature in this season's championship.

We've given you five clues to the identity of each one. Guess it after the first clue, and you get five points, after two clues, and you get four points, and so on.

Once you've finished, add up all your points and see if you can beat your friends to pole position!

CIRCUIT ONE

2 It's 3.194 miles long and drivers must complete sixty laps.

3 It staged the first-ever world championship race in 1950.

4 Famous bends include Maggotts, Becketts and Copse.

5 It has often staged the British Grand Prix.

CIRCUIT TWO

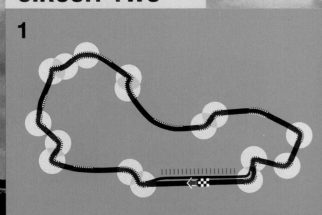

2 It's just over 3.295 miles long and was first used in 1996.

3 The street-based track goes round the shore of a lake.

4 Two of the grandstands are named after this country's most famous ex-drivers, Jack Brabham and Alan Jones.

5 This year it will stage the Australian Grand Prix.

CIRCUIT THREE

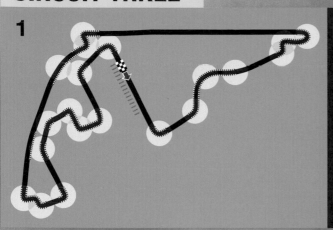

1

2 Set on an island, this tricky, twisting track runs for 3.45 miles.

3 A few lucky guests will be able to sit in the Sun Tower, with the track running right underneath them.

4 It's the second Grand Prix of the season that will be held in the Middle East.

5 It's set to stage the finale of the 2009 season.

CIRCUIT FOUR

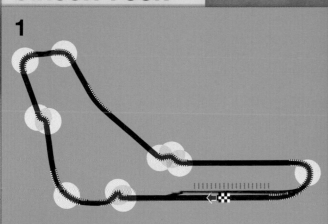

1

2 This track has staged more Grands Prix than any other circuit.

3 It's the oldest European circuit still in permanent use.

4 Several long straights make it one of F1 racing's fastest tracks.

5 The crowd are guaranteed to go berserk if a Black Stallion wins the racc!

CIRCUIT FIVE

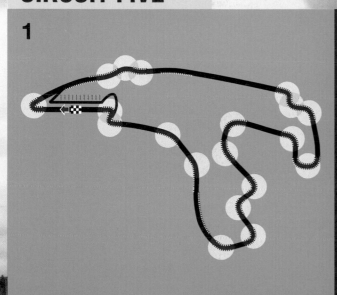

1

2 At 4.352 miles, this is the longest circuit on the calendar – although originally it was over 7 miles long!

3 One of the most challenging tracks going, only the best drivers have ever mastered it. No surprise then that Michael Schumacher has won six times here!

4 The track is set on the edge of the beautiful Ardennes mountains.

5 When F1 cars aren't tearing round it, the track is a normal road, hence the brilliantly named Bus Stop chicane!

SPOT THE DIFFERENCE

Here are two pictures of Lewis Hamilton holding aloft the Belgian Grand Prix™ trophy. But can you spot the ten things that are different in picture A from picture B?

CONSTRUCTOR CONUNDRUMS

This season there are ten teams taking part in the Constructors' World Championship. Can you unravel these anagrams to find out their names?

1 A brews bum

___ _____

2 Roots or so

____ _____

3 Ciao friend

_____ _____

4 Idler lung crab

___ ____ _____

5 Wail slim

_____

6 Oat toy

_____

7 Rare fir

_____

8 Scarce led mermen

_____ _____

9 Real nut

_____

10 GB Prawn

_____ __

A DAY IN THE LIFE OF AN F1™ DRIVER

Our top newshound, Speed Merchant, has gained exclusive access to the diary of former F1™ golden boy, Max Bloated, who retired at the end of last season. Here, in an exclusive extract from his forthcoming book, Podium Highs, he reveals what it's like to be part of the Formula One™ in-crowd.

...The British Grand Prix™, 2008

6.00 am
The alarm goes. It's race day and time for a light breakfast, an hour in the gym and then a good five-mile run to blow the cobwebs away.

6.01 am
Suddenly I remember I was at a promoter's party last night . . . till quite late. Fall back to sleep.

11.07 am
Wake up again in a complete panic. The race starts in just under two hours. Disaster!

11.10 am
Check phone. I've got sixty-five messages from the team boss. He doesn't seem very happy.

11.11 am
I convince myself I've gone deaf before remembering I've got earplugs in. And that accounts for the fact I didn't hear anyone hammering away on the door of my luxury motor home.

11.50 am
Having eaten a full English breakfast, I shower and start to prepare myself for the race by playing a few games on my PlayStation.

12.30 pm
Make my way down to the pits.

1.00 pm
And we're off! Well, everybody else is, but I seem to have stalled the car. All I can hear is the team boss raging down the radio at me. He really can be a very rude man.

1.15 pm

I'm last and I've already been lapped by the three leading cars. Things aren't looking good. And what's more, that fry-up is playing havoc with my insides.

1.58 pm

I'd always wondered what the red button on the side of the steering wheel did but perhaps now wasn't the time to find out. The engine seems to have stopped!

2.15 pm

Great, I've just overtaken someone!

2.16 pm

Whoops, it was the safety car! Everyone seems to be waving flags at me, and don't look very happy.

2.48 pm

The boss has been on again. I've got a drive-through penalty which means I have to go through the pit lane when I'm next passing. I wonder if I'll have time to make a quick loo stop, too.

2.55 pm

I can see the chequered flag. Unfortunately, seventeen other cars have already seen it and it looks like I'm last. Again. But hey, let's look on the bright side – at least I finished.

5.06 pm

Unbelievable. I've been disqualified! Apparently the car was riding too low and scraping the track. Must have been that fry-up I ate.

7.10 pm

Nobody seems to be speaking to me.

7.55 pm

I'm back at the pits looking for my phone. I'm sure I left it here somewhere. Why's it gone all dark? "Hey, don't shut the door, I'm in here!"

8.01 pm

I'm locked in, it's cold and my phone is dead, too. I wonder what time they open up in the morning . . .

TRACK TEASER

Here's another test for your brain cells. First you have to solve the clues and then write your answers in the grid opposite. Once you've done that, rearrange the letters in the grey boxes to spell out the name of a famous racetrack.

CLUES

1 He replaced Vettel at Toro Rosso
2 Top Spanish speed-meister
3 Father and son who have both won the World Drivers' Championship
4 Name for the tyres all F1 cars now use
5 Trackside flag waver
6 Colour of the lights that must go out before a Grand Prix can start
7 Country that Robert Kubica calls home
8 Type of design that makes the car go faster
9 The only Frenchman to win the drivers' title
10 First name of the man who founded Ferrari
11 He won BMW Sauber's only Grand Prix in 2008

THE NAME OF THE HIDDEN RACETRACK IS:

PERFECT MATCH

It's not often we get to see the faces of our F1™ heroes – more often than not all we see is their eyes peering out from underneath their helmets.

So, can you identify the drivers below from their helmets and eyes alone? To help you, there's a bit of a cryptic clue for each one.

1. Drove a Ferrari to the title in 2004.
2. Many F1 experts consider him to be the greatest driver of all time.
3. He won the Australian Grand Prix in 2009.
4. Top British driver who retired at the end of the 2008 season.
5. He was born in Stevenage in 1985.
6. New to the Red Bull team in 2009 and tipped for a bright future.

WINNERS WORD SEARCH

Can you spot the names of the last ten winners
of the F1™ championship in the grid below?

```
N M R O C W E D T O M N B V C
A I E U A P H O I U Y T R E W
B Z T S E N N A D C H B M I T
R C R G E C I G K G A L G V G
O B J A S J F W O K M J J I J
I M P H I L L H U H I H H L H
L E U I E K O S U E L N E L E
L V N L N N K N T N T N E E N
P N W I V A L O N S O D G N N
X P A F S L F E N F N P S E F
K R E E V S P T P E X N P U P
H O Y E R T Y U O F N P O V O
U S C H U M A C H E R C D E C
O T M R T M A N S E L L Y U I
C V W T I S N A L W O V P V X
```

Alonso

Räikkönen

Schumacher

Hamilton

Hill

Hakkinen

Villeneuve

Prost

Mansell

Senna

COPY BOOK

How good are your drawing skills? Can you copy this picture of Jenson Button taking the chequered flag at the Australian Grand Prix™ in 2009?

IT'S A FAMILY AFFAIR

It's amazing how many father and son combos – and a pair of brothers – have taken to Formula One™ racing track.

Draw a line to match the duo on the left with the correct family name on the right.

1. DAMON AND GRAHAM

2. NELSON AND NELSINHO

3. RALF AND MICHAEL (BROTHERS)

4. GILLES AND JACQUES

5. KEKE AND NICO

6. MARIO AND MICHAEL

7. JACK AND DAVID

A) PIQUET

B) ROSBERG

C) VILLENEUVE

D) ANDRETTI

E) SCHUMACHER

F) BRABHAM

G) HILL

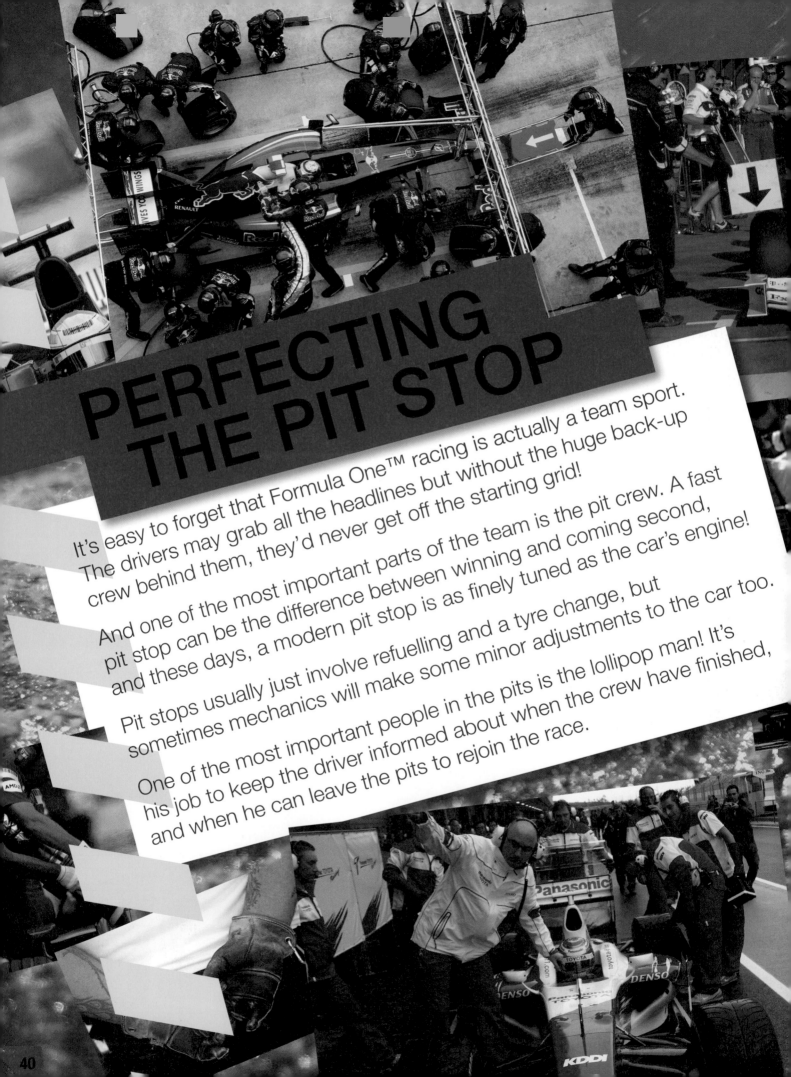

PERFECTING THE PIT STOP

It's easy to forget that Formula One™ racing is actually a team sport. The drivers may grab all the headlines but without the huge back-up crew behind them, they'd never get off the starting grid!

And one of the most important parts of the team is the pit crew. A fast pit stop can be the difference between winning and coming second, and these days, a modern pit stop is as finely tuned as the car's engine!

Pit stops usually just involve refuelling and a tyre change, but sometimes mechanics will make some minor adjustments to the car too.

One of the most important people in the pits is the lollipop man! It's his job to keep the driver informed about when the crew have finished, and when he can leave the pits to rejoin the race.

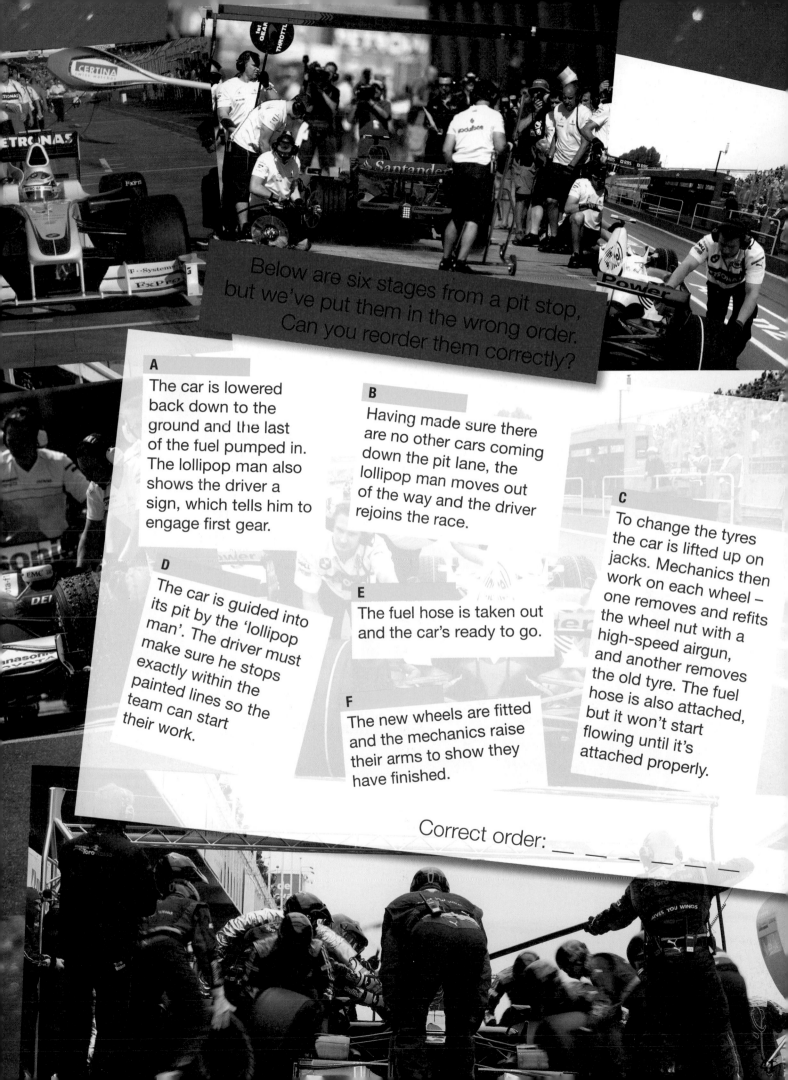

Below are six stages from a pit stop, but we've put them in the wrong order. Can you reorder them correctly?

A

The car is lowered back down to the ground and the last of the fuel pumped in. The lollipop man also shows the driver a sign, which tells him to engage first gear.

B

Having made sure there are no other cars coming down the pit lane, the lollipop man moves out of the way and the driver rejoins the race.

C

To change the tyres the car is lifted up on jacks. Mechanics then work on each wheel – one removes and refits the wheel nut with a high-speed airgun, and another removes the old tyre. The fuel hose is also attached, but it won't start flowing until it's attached properly.

D

The car is guided into its pit by the 'lollipop man'. The driver must make sure he stops exactly within the painted lines so the team can start their work.

E

The fuel hose is taken out and the car's ready to go.

F

The new wheels are fitted and the mechanics raise their arms to show they have finished.

Correct order: ___ ___ ___ ___ ___ ___

HOW TO SPOT A FUTURE F1™

So, do you reckon you can spot a future F1™ champ?

A chap called Richard Hopkins certainly can. He saw his son competing against a 13-year-old Lewis Hamilton in a go-kart race and was so impressed, he placed a series of bets that Lewis would win his first Grand Prix™ by the age of 23, and another that he would be World Champion by the age of 25. And thanks to his hunch, he's now £125,000 richer! So if you've got a younger brother – or sister – and they do any of the following, start placing your bets!

Their first word is 'Nürburgring'.

They sleep in a crash helmet made out of an old saucepan.

They manage to negotiate a deal with a major oil company to sponsor their romper suit.

They can ride their three-wheeler bike before they can actually walk.

Every time they do any colouring, it comes out looking like a chequered flag.

At nursery school, instead of drinking their milk, they insist on standing up on a chair and spraying it over everyone.

By their fifth birthday they've already rebuilt the engine in your dad's car.

You catch them giving the dog a stop-go penalty after the poor mutt cuts them up on the stairs.

By the time they reach primary school they've already passed their driving test.

WINNER

43

FORMULA ONE™ CALENDAR 2009

The 2009 season should really be hotting up by now! Here's a list of all the races for you to complete. You can now plot the final few months of the season too, as the drama really starts to unfold!

March 29
2009 FORMULA 1 ING AUSTRALIAN GRAND PRIX (Melbourne)
Winner:

April 5
2009 FORMULA 1 PETRONAS MALAYSIAN GRAND PRIX
(Kuala Lumpur)
Winner:

April 19
2009 FORMULA 1 CHINESE GRAND PRIX (Shanghai)
Winner:

April 26
2009 FORMULA 1 GULF AIR BAHRAIN GRAND PRIX (Sakhir)
Winner:

May 10
FORMULA 1 GRAN PREMIO DE ESPANA TELEFONICA 2009
(Catalunya)
Winner:

May 24
FORMULA 1 GRAND PRIX DE MONACO 2009 (Monte Carlo)
Winner:

June 7
2009 FORMULA 1 ING TURKISH GRAND PRIX (Istanbul)
Winner:

June 21
2009 FORMULA 1 SANTANDER BRITISH GRAND PRIX
(Silverstone)
Winner:

July 12
*FORMULA 1 GROSSER PREIS SANTANDER VON
DEUTSCHLAND 2009* (Nürburgring)
Winner:

July 26
FORMULA 1 ING MAGYAR NAGYDIJ 2009 (Budapest)
Winner:

August 23
2009 FORMULA 1 TELEFONICA GRAND PRIX OF EUROPE
(Valencia)
Winner:

August 30
2009 FORMULA 1 ING BELGIAN GRAND PRIX
(Spa-Francorchamps)
Winner:

September 13
FORMULA 1 GRAN PREMIO SANTANDER D'ITALIA 2009
(Monza)
Winner:

September 27
2009 FORMULA 1 SINGTEL SINGAPORE GRAND PRIX
(Singapore)
Winner:

October 4
2009 FORMULA 1 FUJI TELEVISION JAPANESE GRAND PRIX
(Suzuka)
Winner:

October 18
FORMULA 1 GRANDE PREMIO DO BRASIL 2009 (Sao Paulo)
Winner:

November 1
2009 FORMULA 1 ETIHAD AIRWAYS ABU DHABI GRAND PRIX
(Yas Marina Circuit)
Winner:

DEADLINE DILEMMA

No sooner had gifted but clumsy F1™ reporter Speed Merchant finished interviewing five of this year's championship contenders than he dropped his notebook, scattering the precious pages everywhere.

Can you match Speed's notes to the correct F1™ star and help him meet his deadline?

1. "Finnish ace who lived up to his iceman nickname by topping the podium twice last season, with wins in the Spanish and Malaysian Grands Prix."

2. "Recently snapped up by the Red Bull team after a blistering second half of last season with Toro Rosso, this exciting young German driver is tipped for great things."

3. "After a disappointing 2008 season, could this be the year that he finally steps out of his father's shadow and takes Williams back to the top?"

4. "It just wasn't to be for this talented driver last year but with his Ferrari purring nicely, who's to say he won't become the first Brazilian since the great Ayrton Senna to clinch the title in 2009?"

5. "Last season, the F1 world was forced to sit up and take notice of this flying Pole, who turned the form book upside down by clinching fourth place in the Championship with a phenomenal 75 points."

Answers:

1.

2.

3.

4.

5.

The 2009 season features seventeen circuits from around the world. We've jumbled up the names of ten of them. Can you work out which is which?

1. Evilness Rot

_ _ _ _ _ _ _ _ _ _ _

2. Scarf Champ Aprons

_ _ _ _ _ _ _ _ _ _ _ _ _ _ _ _ _

3. Clean Motor

_ _ _ _ _ _ _ _ _ _ _

4. Snail Tub

_ _ _ _ _ _ _ _

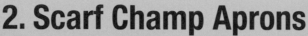

5. Burr Grin Gün

_ _ _ _ _ _ _ _ _ _ _

6. A Lacy Aunt

_ _ _ _ _ _ _ _ _

7. Rumble One

_ _ _ _ _ _ _ _ _

8. A Hag Shin

_ _ _ _ _ _ _ _

9. Opera Sing

_ _ _ _ _ _ _ _ _

10. Airman Say

_ _ _ _ _ _ _ _ _

FORMULA ONE™

FABULOUS FACTS AND FEARSOME FIGURES

It's rumoured that the new Shanghai Circuit in China cost over £200 million to build!

On each Renault car there are sixty-seven sponsor stickers, each costing £350 a set.

Since 1950, a total of forty-five drivers have been killed while driving in a F1 race. No drivers have been involved in a fatal accident since 1994.

Carbon fibre, the stuff used to make F1 wings so sturdy, is thirteen times thinner than the average human hair and seven times stronger than steel.

It takes two mechanics about four days to put an F1 engine together.

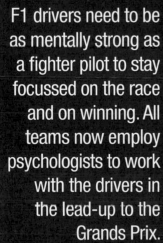

F1 drivers need to be as mentally strong as a fighter pilot to stay focussed on the race and on winning. All teams now employ psychologists to work with the drivers in the lead-up to the Grands Prix.

Force India takes ninety-six headsets, forty-four bottles of champagne, forty race suits and 1,600 litres of fuel to each Grand Prix!

Over 600 million people worldwide watched the F1 season unfold in 2008.

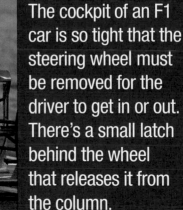

The cockpit of an F1 car is so tight that the steering wheel must be removed for the driver to get in or out. There's a small latch behind the wheel that releases it from the column.

The Chinese are now the world's greatest F1 fans, with over 119 million people tuning in to watch.

10 FORMULA ONE™ FINISHES OF ALL TIME

There have been some right humdinger finishes over the years, with cars going for it neck and neck right to the finish line. We've come up with a list of the ten closest ever – but do you think there'll ever be a dead heat in a Grand Prix™?

1954

French Grand Prix™:
Juan Manuel Fangio beat Karl Kling by 0.1 seconds

A race from the early days of Formula One racing, Fangio clung on against the German Kling, only just managing to defeat him.

1955

British Grand Prix™:
Stirling Moss beat Juan Manuel Fangio by 0.2 seconds

A close shave for top British driver Stirling Moss, who held on to beat Argentina's Fangio and win his first ever race.

1961

French Grand Prix™:
Giancarlo Baghetti beat Dan Gurney by 0.1 seconds

Italian Baghetti managed to slip past the American, Dan Gurney in the home straight, and claim his first Grand Prix win.

1967

Italian Grand Prix™:
John Surtees beat Jack Brabham by 0.2 seconds

The Monza track was once famed for its close finishes, and they didn't get much closer than this! The Aussie, Brabham, actually managed to overtake Britain's Surtees with the finish line in sight, but unfortunately the inside line he'd taken was covered in cement dust and Surtees was able to regain the lead and take the flag.

1969

Italian Grand Prix™:
Jackie Stewart beat Jochen Rindt by 0.08 seconds

Monza once more, and this time the tenacious Scot, Stewart, left it late to ease past the Austrian Rindt. Stewart went on to win the championship that year.

1971

Italian Grand Prix™:
Peter Gethin beat Ronnie Peterson by 0.01 seconds

Fittingly, the closest ever finish was at the famous Monza circuit, with five drivers flying out of the final corner in with a chance of victory. And it was Britain's Gethin who hung on to win his one and only Grand Prix.

1981

Spanish Grand Prix™:
Gilles Villeneuve beat Jacques Laffite by 0.22 seconds

The skilful Canadian Villeneuve managed to hold off four cars on the line, with Frenchman Laffite crossing in second.

1982

Austrian Grand Prix™:
Elio de Angelis beat Keke Rosberg by 0.05 seconds

Nail-biting stuff as the Italian de Angelis held off the challenge of the Flying Finn Rosberg.

1986

Spanish Grand Prix™:
Ayrton Senna beat Nigel Mansell by 0.014 seconds

Before the Grand Prix the finishing line had been moved closer to the final corner, which made the final straight much shorter. And that did it for our Nige because he was on fire as he tore round that last corner, but he literally ran out of track.

2000

Canadian Grand Prix™:
Michael Schumacher beat Rubens Barrichello by 0.174 seconds

Schumacher was on his way to the first of five championships on the trot, when he held off teammate Barrichello during a very wet Canadian Grand Prix.

LET'S HEAR IT FOR THE GIRLS

The first woman to qualify for a Grand Prix was Italy's Maria Teresa de Filippis, who made her debut in the Belgian Grand Prix in 1958, and went on to qualify for four more races.

The first, and so far only, woman ever to win any F1 points was another Italian, Lella Lombardi. She managed to qualify for an impressive twelve races during the mid 1970s and famously finished sixth at the Spanish Grand Prix in 1975. However, she was only awarded half a point because the race had been cut short due to a crash.

Other famous women drivers include Britain's Divina Galica who, let's face it, was something of a speed freak! As the captain of the British Women's Ski team she competed in three winter Olympics, before swapping skis for wheels and trying her hand at motor racing. She failed to qualify for her one and only home race, the 1976 British Grand Prix, but did carry on racing other cars after leaving F1 racing.

Although South African Desiré Wilson never managed to qualify for a Grand Prix either, she did win a competition involving older F1 cars that was staged at Brands Hatch, and as a result the track still has a stand named after her.

The most recent woman to have a go at F1 racing was another Italian, Giovanna Amati, who, driving a Brabham, failed to qualify for the first three Grands Prix of the 1992 season. She was later replaced by Damon Hill.

But there could soon be a new woman on the block. An American team are apparently planning to enter the 2010 World Championship and many would like to see one of their driving seats go to Danica Patrick, the first woman to ever win an Indy car race in the States.

SPOOF EMAILS

Our roving news hound, Speed Merchant, has been at it again. He's managed to tap into some pretty dramatic emails that have been pinging around the F1™ world. And as ever, he's only too happy to spill the beans!

From: Felipe Massa
To: Lewis Hamilton
Subject: Pizza

Well done Lewis, you thoroughly deserved to win the Championship. How do you fancy meeting up for a pizza and a chinwag?

Your obedient servant,

Felipe

From: Michael Schumacher
To: The Head of Ferrari
Subject: Comeback

Looks like you lot need a bit of help now that Hamilton is flying for McLaren. I'm fed up with driving minicabs in Berlin, so if the price is right, I'd be happy to take on the young Englander.

Anyway must rush, I've got a fare waiting...

Mike

From: Sebastian Vettel
To: FIA Organising Committee
Subject: Champagne

Just a thought, but how about swapping the usual bottle of bubbly on the winner's podium for a can of that power drink everyone loves so much? You know the one I mean... After all, there is a credit crunch on you know.

Yours with wings,

Seb

From: Mick's Garage
To: Head of Engineering, McLaren-Mercedes
Subject: Spark plugs

Alright guv,

Just thought I ought to let you know that we're doing a great '2 for 1' deal on the old sparkos at the moment. Also, if you're interested, I know a geezer who can get his hands on some knock-off diesel. Just a pony for 25 gallons to you, mate.

Cheers,

Micky

FAMOUS F1™ MOMENTS

Formula One™ racing first started in 1950 and since then we've had over half a century of thrills, spills, and incredible excitement. For this challenge, you've got to match up the events in the column on the left with the dates in the column on the right. Some are easy and some are as tricky as the trickiest street circuit you've ever seen!

A	LEWIS HAMILTON BECOMES THE NINTH BRITON TO WIN THE DRIVERS' WORLD CHAMPIONSHIP	1996
B	MICHAEL SCHUMACHER WINS HIS RECORD-BREAKING SIXTH TITLE	1985
C	DAMON HILL IS CROWNED CHAMPION	1982
D	ENZO FERRARI SETS UP THE COMPANY THAT STILL BEARS HIS NAME TODAY	2003
E	LEWIS HAMILTON WAS BORN	1994
F	KEKE ROSBERG BECOMES THE FIRST FINN TO WIN THE CHAMPIONSHIP	1976
G	AYRTON SENNA DIES AT THE SAN MARINO GRAND PRIX	2006
H	FLAMBOYANT BRITISH DRIVER JAMES HUNT IS CHAMPION	2008
I	FERNANDO ALONSO WINS HIS SECOND TITLE	1978
J	THE WILLIAMS TEAM ENTER THEIR FIRST GRAND PRIX	1928

BEST OF BRITISH MAZE

So, who was the greatest-ever British driver? Were things tougher in the 1960s, or do you need even more skill to handle the ultra-powerful cars of today? Let's see if we can find out using this mesmerizing maze. Only one car will make it to the finish. But who will it be?

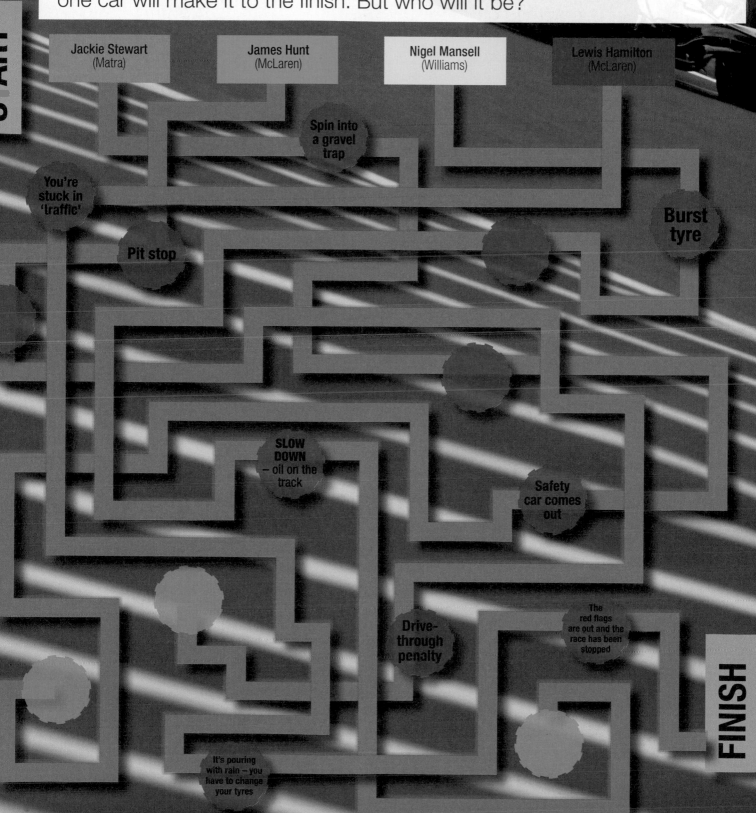

START

FINISH

Jackie Stewart (Matra)

James Hunt (McLaren)

Nigel Mansell (Williams)

Lewis Hamilton (McLaren)

Spin into a gravel trap

You're stuck in 'traffic'

Pit stop

Burst tyre

SLOW DOWN – oil on the track

Safety car comes out

Drive-through penalty

The red flags are out and the race has been stopped

It's pouring with rain – you have to change your tyres

CARDOKU

Here's a Sudoku with a bit of a difference! Study each line, across and down, very carefully. The numbers need to appear once, and only once, in each line going across and each line going down. And to make things even more interesting, each number must only appear in each 'block' once as well. Good luck – you're going to need it!

CROSSWORD

Another testing challenge for all you F1™ fans. Once again there's a real mixture of old and new to get that grey matter working.

ACROSS

1. A very tight bend (7)
2. He won six Grands Prix in 2008 (5)
5. Famous British racetrack (9, 4)
7. Constructor that has entered more races than anyone else (7)
8. The youngest Brit to ever race in a Grand Prix was Jenson ... (6)
11. Top driver from Spain, Fernando ... (6)
12. Famous German driver, Michael ... (10)
13. Youngest ever Grand Prix winner, Sebastian ... (6)

DOWN

1. Last British F1 Champ, Lewis ... (8)
3. Britain's three-time Constructor's World Champion, Jackie ... (7)
4. It comes out on to the track if there's been an accident (6, 3)
6. A place for refuelling and changing tyres (3)
8. Only country in South America to stage a Grand Prix in 2008 (6)
9. Piquet races for this team (7)
10. This country has entered more F1 drivers than any other (3)

F1™ CARS
– ENGINEERING MARVELS

Formula One™ cars are amongst the most complicated feats o engineering ever built – millions of pounds go into developing each one.

From their computer-controlled gearboxes to their futuristic, aerodynami shapes, these speed monsters have more in common with spaceships than the cars you see tootling along the street!

REAR WING

Part of the car which helps to keep the back wheels on the tarmac using a type of force called 'down-force'. The engineers have to get the angle of the wing spot on, because it also causes 'drag', and too much drag will slow the car down.

ENGINE

All Formula One cars have 2.4 litre V8 engines that can hit 18,000 rpm. Put another way, they can chuck out eight times more power than your average family saloon!

FUEL TANK

This sits behind the driver and is made of super strong Kevlar to prevent it from being punctured.

DIFFUSER

Another clever device, it takes the air passing underneath the car at the front and sends it shooting out at the back.

SIDEPOD

These big air scoops on each side of the cockpit help out with the aerodynamics and also house the car's radiators.

CHASSIS

This is the part of the car that things like th engine and suspension system are attache to, so it's quite important! It also includes the driver's cockpit, so it goes through very rigorous safety tests before it's passed as C to use. Made of carbon fibre, it is immense strong to protect the driver in a crash, but i also designed so that everything attached t it breaks off if there is a smash.

GEARBOX

An F1 car has seven gears, which can be changed in milliseconds. The driver changes gear using special buttons or paddles on his steering wheel.

SKID BLOCK

This is a 1cm strip fixed to the underside of the car. It stops cars gaining an unfair advantage by running too close to the track surface – remember, milliseconds count in F1. If the skid block is less than 9mm by the end of the race, the car may be disqualified!

FRONT WING

This is crucial as it's the first part of the car that comes into contact with the air. It helps to ensure the air flows over the car efficiently and so doesn't affect its speed too much.

TYRES

Tyres have more impact on the speed of the car than anything else. In 2009 all the teams have been using 'slick tyres' which have no tread on them and give the best possible grip in dry conditions. If it does start raining, the pit crews also have special grooved, wet weather tyres.

STEERING WHEEL

This is one of the most complex pieces of kit in the car. It has digital displays as well as buttons that control everything from gear changes to the mix of fuel going through to the engine.

SUSPENSION

This helps make for a smoother ride because, let's face it, you know about it if you go over a bump at 300km/h!

BRAKES

Nowadays these are made from carbon fibre discs that glow when the driver applies them. Mind you, you'd get a bit red in the face if you were capable of slowing a car down from 300km/h to 80km/h in just two seconds!

ANSWERS

Pages 8–9 1. True – nine Brits have won the championship. 2. True. 3. False – he was from Brazil. 4. True. 5. True. 6. False – they're all from Germany. 7. False – it was a McLaren. 8. True. 9. True – Massa won 6, Hamilton 5. 10. True 11. False – it's just 78. 12. True. 13. False – it was Sutil and Giancarlo Fisichella. 14. True. 15. False – Rubens Barrichello is older, born in 1972. 16. False – Hunt won by over 18 seconds. 17. False – South Africa staged its last Grand Prix in 1993. 18. False – they're all from Finland. 19. True. 20. True.

Page 12 Brazil: Ayrton Senna; Great Britain: Lewis Hamilton; Italy: Monza; USA: Indianapolis; Argentina: Juan Manuel Fangio; Germany: Nürburgring; Finland: Mika Hakkinen; Australia: Albert Park; France: Alain Prost; Austria: Niki Lauda

Pages 16–17 1. A; 2. C; 3. B; 4. C; 5. B; 6. A; 7. B; 8. B; 9. C; 10. B.

Pages 28–29 Circuit One: Silverstone, UK. Circuit Two: Albert Park, Melbourne, Australia. Circuit Three: Yas Marina Circuit, Abu Dhabi. Circuit Four: Monza, Italy. Circuit Five: Spa-Francorchamps, Belgium.

Page 29 1. Renault. 2. Ferrari. 3. Red Bull Racing. 4. Toyota. 5. Williams. 6. McLaren. 7. Toro Rosso. 8. BMW Sauber. 9. Force India

Page 30 Spot the difference

Page 31
1 BMW Sauber
2 Toro Rosso
3 Force India
4 Red Bull Racing
5 Williams
6 Toyota
7 Ferrari
8 McLaren Mercedes
9 Renault
10 Brawn GP

Page 35

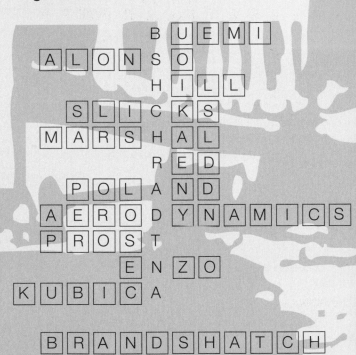

Page 36 1. E – Michael Schumacher; 2. C – Ayrton Senna; 3. F – Jenson Button; 4. A – David Coulthard; 5. B – Lewis Hamilton; 6. D – Sebastian Vettel.

```
N M R O C W E D T O M N B V C
A I E U A P H O I U Y T R E W
B Z T S E N N A D C H B M I T
R C R G E C I G K G A L G V G
O B J A S J F W O K M J J I J
I M P H I L L H U H I H H L H
L E U I E K O S U E L N E L E
L V N L N N K N T N T N E N N
P N W I V A L O N S O D G N N
X P A F S L F E N F N P S E F
K R E E V S P T P E X N P U P
H O Y E R T Y U O F N P O V O
U S C H U M A C H E R C D E C
O T M R T M A N S E L L Y U I
C V W T I S N A L W O V P V X
```

age 39

G; 2. A; 3. E; 4. C; 5. B; 6. D; 7. F.

age 41

orrect order: D, C, F, A, E, B

age 45

C, Kimi Räikkönen
D, Sebastian Vettel
B, Nico Rosberg
A, Felipe Massa
E, Robert Kubica

age 46

Silverstone
Spa-Francorchamps
Monte Carlo
Istanbul
Nürburgring
Catalunya
Melbourne
Shanghai
Singapore
. Yas Marina

Page 54

A) 2008
B) 2003
C) 1996
D) 1928
E) 1985
F) 1982
G) 1994
H) 1976
I) 2006
J) 1978

Page 55

Lewis Hamilton

Page 56

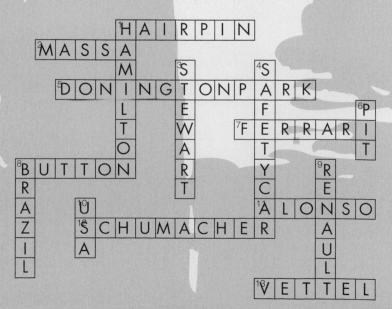

Page 57